EARLY INTERMEDIATE

Ocean Scenes

6 ORIGINAL PIANO SOLOS ~~~~~~~~ ell

Ocean scenes always draw me in

to remember,

to hear,

to believe...

ISBN 978-1-4234-8927-6

WILLIS MUSIC

Exclusively Distributed By

HAL•LEONARD®
CORPORATION

7777 W. BLUEMOUND RD. P.O. BOX 13819 MILWAUKEE, WI 53213

Visit Hal Leonard Online at
www.halleonard.com

CONTENTS

First Comes the Sun

First comes the sun,
moving silently from a distant shore.

Randall Hartsell

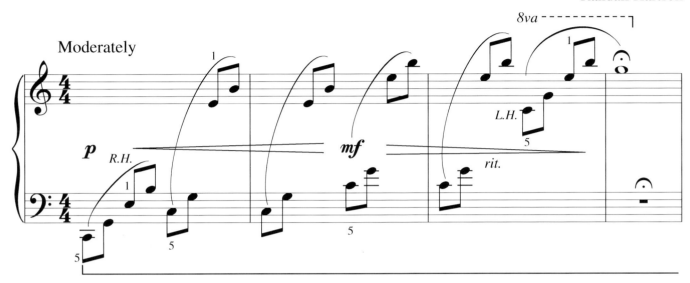

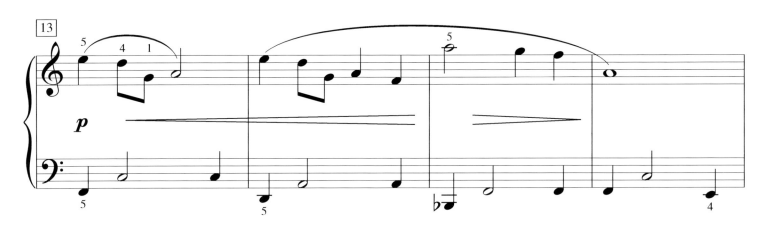

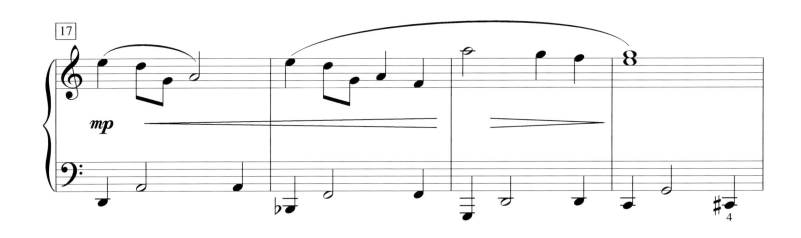

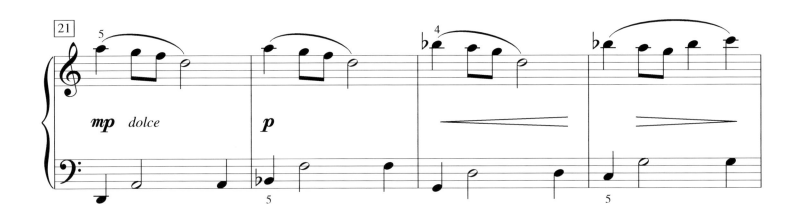

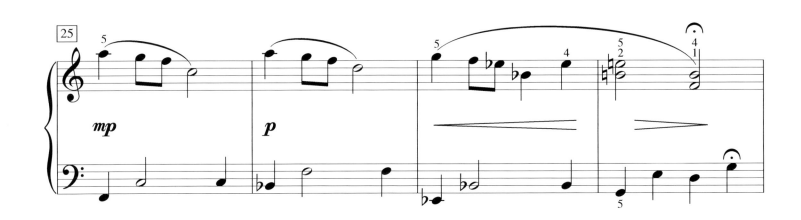

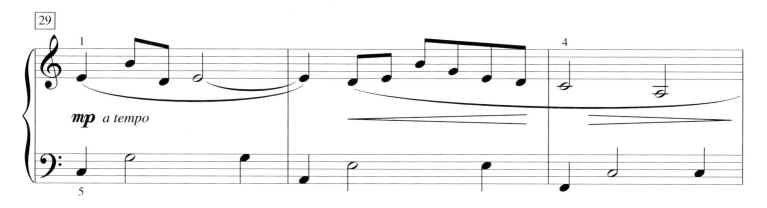

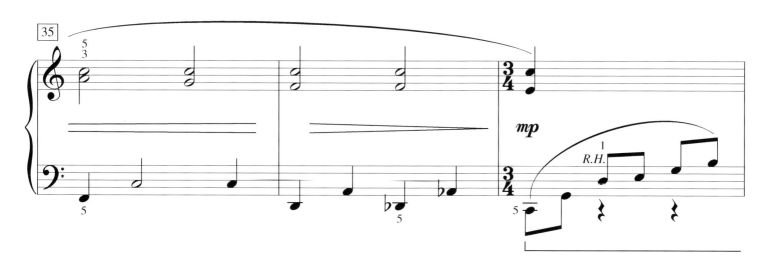

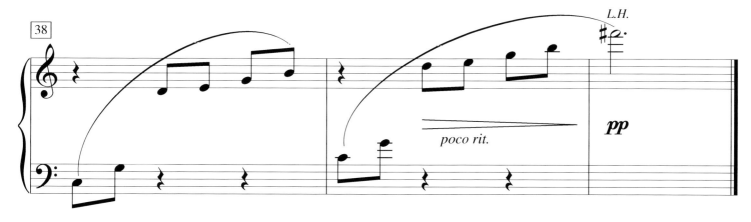

Sitting by the Sea

Come and sit beside the sea,
as you share a day with me,
and we look across the waves.

Randall Hartsell

Moving with energy

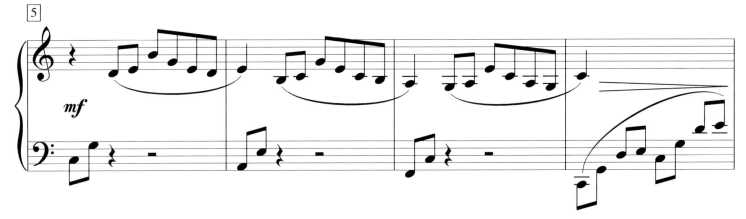

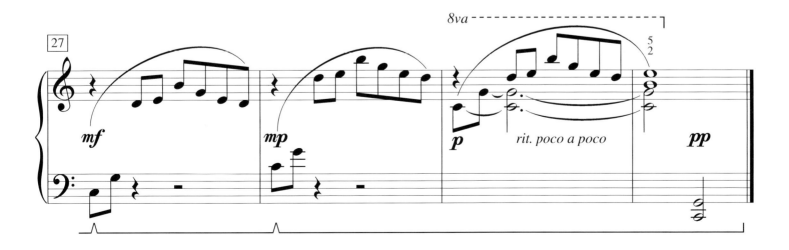

Bay Breezes

*Breezes blowing, never knowing
how they're coming,
where they're going.*

Randall Hartsell

Moderately, expressively

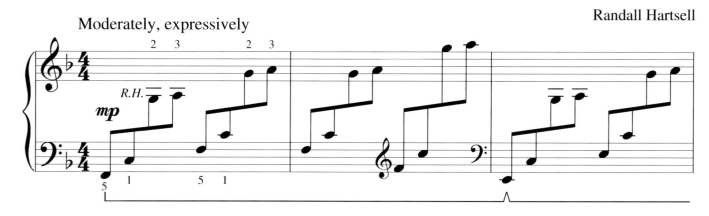

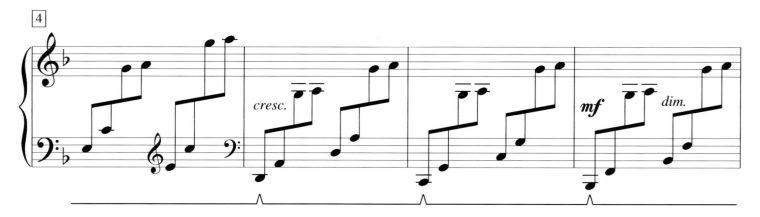

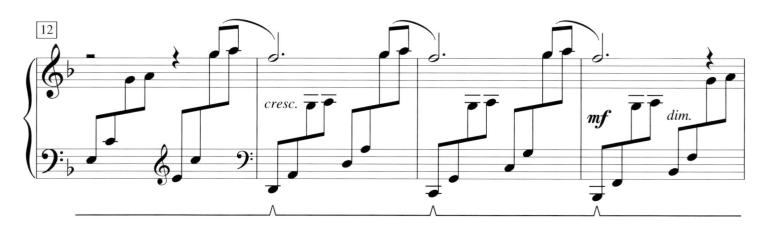

Majestic Waves

Majestic waves of power,
fulfill an endless hour.

Randall Hartsell

Moderately, with intensity

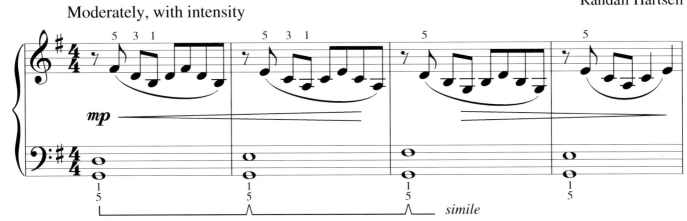

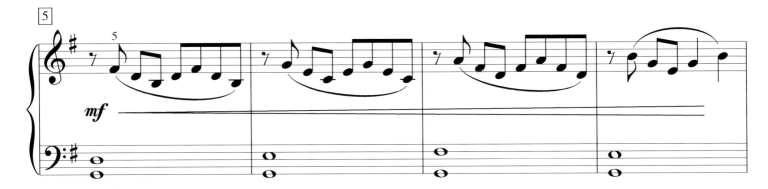

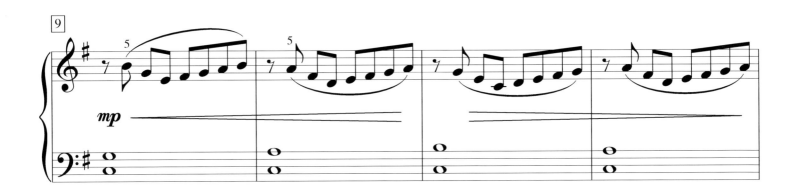

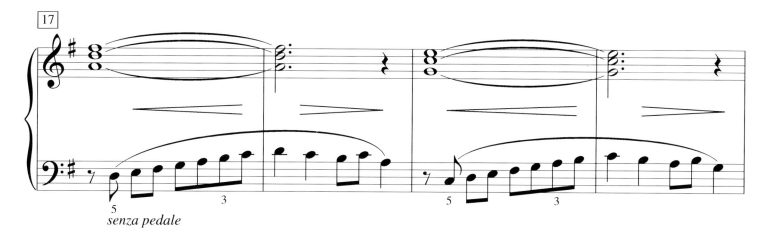

senza pedale

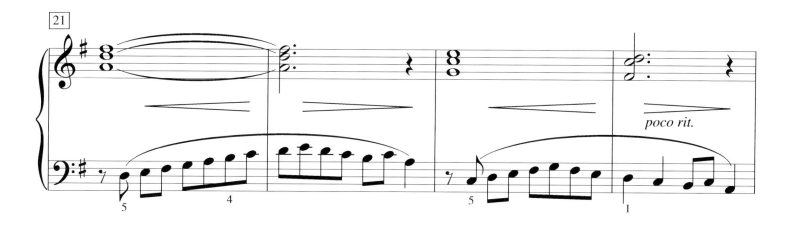

poco rit.

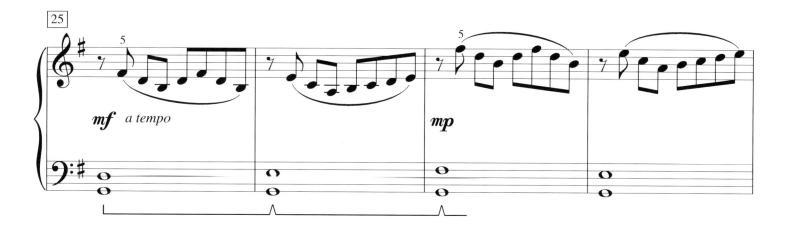

mf   a tempo   mp

p   p

rit. poco a poco

Unexpected Storm

An unexpected streak of light
breaks free to cross the depths of night.

Randall Hartsell

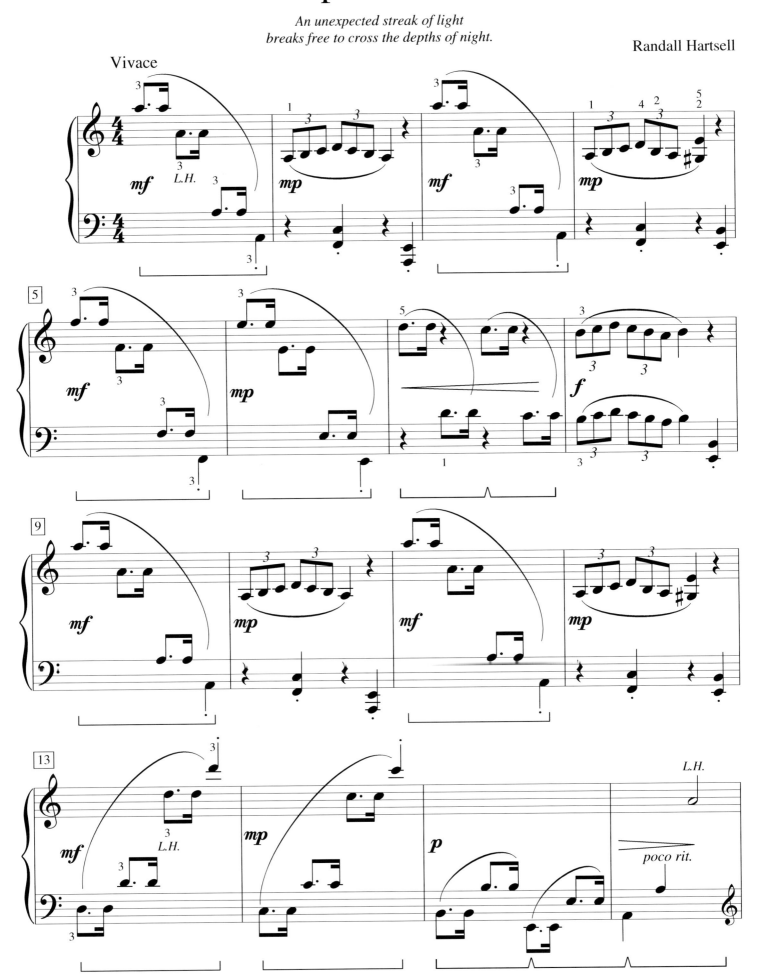

*Start glissando slow, with optional pedal, and accelerate to the end.

Sailing Summer Seas

Sailing summer seas,
Rolling up our sleeves,
Greeting what may come...

Randall Hartsell

Moderately, freely

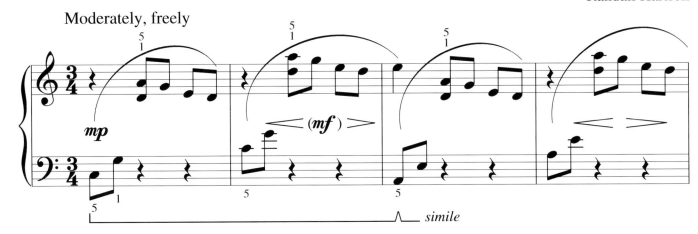

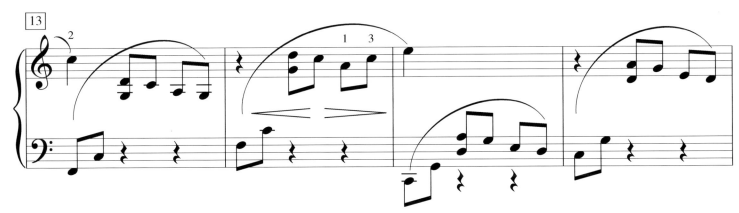

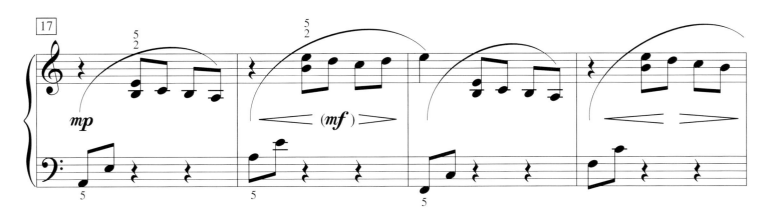

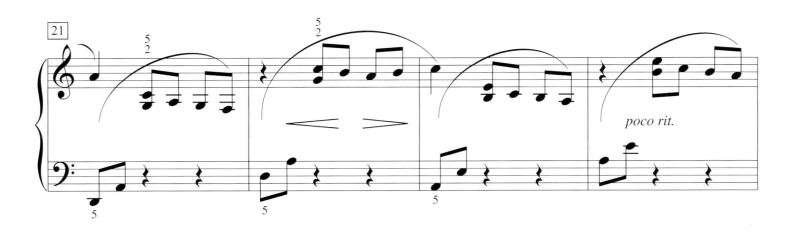

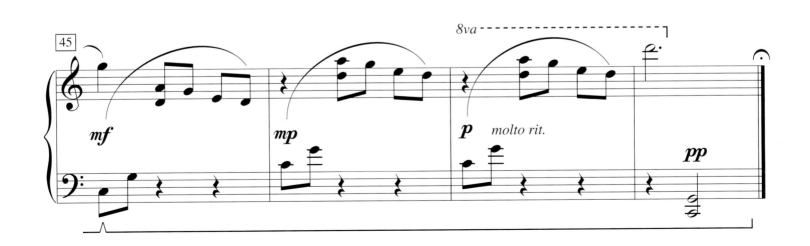